Four Faces of Christian Ministry

Four Faces of Christian Ministry

Essays in honor of
A. DALE FIERS

Essays by

Granville T. Walker
David M. Stowe
Eugene Carson Blake
Ben M. Herbster

With a biographical essay by
Robert L. Friedly

THE BETHANY PRESS • ST. LOUIS, MO.

© *1973 by The Bethany Press*

Library of Congress Cataloging in Publication Data

Main entry under title:
Four faces of Christian ministry.

  CONTENTS: Friedly, R. L. A. Dale Fiers: our first
general minister and president.—Walker, G. T. On the
pastoral ministry.—Stowe, D. M. World responsibilities
for American Christians? [etc.]
  1. Theology—Addresses, essays, lectures. 2. Fiers,
Alan Dale. I. Fiers, Alan Dale. II. Walker,
Granville T.
BR50.F63   253   73-9560
ISBN 0-8272-1005-1

Scripture quotations, unless otherwise noted, are from the Revised
Standard Version of the Bible, copyrighted 1946 and 1952 by the
Division of Christian Education, National Council of the Churches of
Christ in the U.S.A., and used by permission.

Distributed by The G. R. Welch Company, Toronto, Ontario, Canada.

MANUFACTURED IN THE UNITED STATES OF AMERICA

Contents

5

Foreword

AT THIS POINT in the twentieth century, ministry has many faces. Effective ministry, however, will face in one or more broad directions.

Today Christians, individually and in their congregational life, need the priestly and prophetic ministry of a man of God if faith is to be life-giving. The world beyond the church, uncertain of its values, torn with strife, and haunted by a sense of meaninglessness, desperately needs the healing ministry of God's Spirit. The church itself, hampered by division in its effort to serve the one Lord, requires the ministry of the true ecumenical spirit. A ministry which looks toward the needs of individuals, the church itself, and a suffering world, must find new organizational forms to communicate the ancient truths of the Christian gospel in a new age.

Great ministries of our time have had one or another of these faces. Rarely, however, are these four faces of ministry so clearly seen in the ministry of one man as in the case of Dr. A. Dale Fiers. The units of the Christian Church (Disciples of Christ) present this *festschrift, Four Faces of Christian Ministry,* as one token of their love and esteem for a man who has set his face steadfastly toward Jerusalem.

ORVILLE W. WAKE

Robert L. Friedly is executive director of the Office of Communication of the Christian Church (Disciples of Christ), which handles public relations, news, and broadcasting for the church. Winner of the Associated Press Frank C. Allen Award for outstanding newspaper reporting in Louisiana and Mississippi in 1964, Friedly joined the general staff of the church in 1966. He is a member of the board of Religion in American Life, serves on interpretation committees of the National and World Councils of Churches, and has been acting communication officer of the Consultation on Church Union. He chaired the 1971 Institute on Modern Religious Communication Dilemmas at Syracuse University and was part of the fraternal team of Disciples that visited Asia in 1972.

Born in Moundsville, West Virginia, July 2, 1933, Friedly earned the B.A. degree in journalism at Marshall University. He was a copy editor on the **Charleston** (W. Va.) **Gazette,** editor of a Navy newspaper in Atsugi, Japan, and reporter and marine columnist for the **New Orleans States-Item.** He was New Orleans correspondent for **Business Week** magazine.

An active churchman, Friedly has been an elder and has served in other capacities in local congregations. He is married to the former Cecilia Young of Morgan City, Louisiana, and they have three children.

A. Dale Fiers:
Our First General Minister
and President

ROBERT L. FRIEDLY

"INDECISION," the young preacher said, "robs men of influence and makes them a force for evil instead of good."

He was a husky twenty-three-year-old, preaching to his first congregation. A former college football star, he undoubtedly was aware of his own leadership capabilities, but Alan Dale Fiers hardly could have known in 1930 the momentous decisions he would be called upon by his church to face.

For a quarter of a century in one of the most decisive periods in the history of the Christian Church (Disciples of Christ), Dale Fiers would be in a key leadership position. Perhaps no individual since Alexander Campbell would be more front and center in such a shaping period.

The concept of "foreign" missions would change, with a partnership between the church in North America and churches abroad replacing the old managerial paternalism.

The church would be confronted with the social revolution and the cries of people for freedom from oppression.

Disciples would opt for a major restructuring, to express that they are a "church" and not just a collection of congregations and agencies, and to inaugurate a representative assembly, something Campbell sought unsuccessfully in Cincinnati in 1849.

The church would play a leading role in the ecumenical movement and plunge seriously into church union negotiations, following the vision of Campbell, who saw cooperation and federation as necessary steps to organic unity, and unity as the Disciples' unique mission.

9

A. Dale Fiers was born December 17, 1906, in Kankakee, Illinois. His father was a contractor, his mother an ordained minister who rode a horse and buggy circuit in eastern Illinois and western Indiana.

Four-year-old Dale trooped down the aisle during one of his mother's sermons and, on her orders, sat on the corner of the rostrum until she finished. Family responsibilities ended Mother Fiers' ministerial career, but she told her son hopefully, "Someday maybe God will give us a minister in the family."

With his mother and father and two older sisters, Dale Fiers moved to West Palm Beach, Florida, where his father built buildings, including churches, and became mayor of suburban Lake Park, and where Dale, at the age of nine, was baptized by J. H. Bulfin.

In his early years Dale Fiers made it clear to schoolmates that he intended to be a preacher and they "admired him for it," says Judge Banzai Currie, one of the schoolmates. Together they hunted, fished, and tramped along the beach, searching for turtle eggs.

At West Palm Beach High School, Dale—who weighed 170 pounds—starred in baseball, football, basketball, and track. A fullback, he was named to the 1924 Florida All-State Scholastic Football Team.

Teammates, who called Fiers "Casey," say he flunked locker room language. His best expletives were "jeepers creepers" and "gosh hang it."

He made his commitment to full-time Christian work when he was a high school freshman. Then, because of his love of athletics, he went through a period of deep inner conflict about the decision, finally settling it with such resolve that he turned in his semi-pro East Coast League baseball uniform and quit the team when told by the coach he would have to play on Sunday. The coach, shaken, called and urged him to return. He did. And he never played Sunday games.

Upon the recommendation of his pastor, J. H. Bristor, Dale Fiers chose Alexander Campbell's institution, Bethany College, to further his education and in 1925 he enrolled in the West Virginia school. He wore a big raccoon coat and joined Beta Theta Pi. He was only an average student, in his own words, but later was to win some honors at Yale.

Fiers played every minute of every varsity football game his freshman year. At that time Bethany played such powers as Fordham and Pitt. The 195-pounder captained the 1928 team and thirty years later was cited by the *Pittsburgh Press* as the all-time great Bethany fullback. Football, baseball, and track earned him the Tri-State Conference Outstanding Athlete Award.

Dale Fiers was graduated with the bachelor of arts degree in 1929, and on June 11 he and a group of others were ordained at the old Bethany church, during the centennial year of the church's founding by Campbell.

His initial pastorate was First Christian Church in Shadyside, Ohio, a tiny town nestled between the hills and along the Ohio River just south of Wheeling. As yet unmarried, he took a room with a church couple who lived temporarily in the parsonage. He was mature, they remember, relating well to young and old alike. He was a hard worker. And a good preacher.

Fiers' athletic reputation made him particularly attractive to young people. The Young Men's Class grew in attendance sixfold in three months. He rented a house for a youth club, but that venture fell through as the depression dried up funds.

Fiers identified deeply with the problems of people. Mrs. Clarence Gillespie, the landlady, says he prayed all night in his room during particularly difficult periods.

He limited himself to two dates a week, though he talked enough about a Wheeling High School secretary that the landlady invited her over for lemonade and ice cream.

On June 14, 1931, Dale and Betty Kunz were married in Wheeling and they left for Yale, he to seek a divinity degree, she to audit courses. There, Dale Fiers was president of the Campbell Club, won Mersick Awards for preaching and for public reading of scripture, and did some football coaching.

Earning the bachelor of divinity degree in 1935, Fiers accepted a call from High Street Christian Church in Hamilton, Ohio, where he remained four years and where the Fierses' first child, Barbara, was born.

During this period he began accepting invitations from the United Christian Missionary Society to serve as dean of regional youth conferences in the East and South.

In 1939 Fiers accepted the pastorate of Central Christian Church, Newark, Ohio. There, the Fierses' second child, Alan Dale, Jr., was born. Alan was to follow in his father's cleat-steps, playing tackle on an Ohio State University team that won national ranking.

During the World War II years, Dale Fiers headed the Newark Ministerial Association, served on the YMCA Board, and chaired disaster relief for civil defense. He was named in 1944 to his first national post—membership on the Board of Higher Education of the Disciples.

In the summer of 1945 he took refresher courses at Union Theological Seminary in New York. That fall Fiers was called to the Euclid Avenue Christian Church, Cleveland.

Early in his days at Euclid Avenue, Fiers appeared on the Pennsylvania state convention program with P. H. Welshimer, noted restorationist speaker in the Campbell movement.

Welshimer maintained that restoration of the New Testament church was a clear and simple process, and the road Disciples should follow, not "an amalgamation of sects, not a federation of different religious bodies." But Fiers asserted that the world needs a united church and that Disciples could have a conspicuous part in making it a reality. "We must," he said, "share our convictions with strength and humility—the humility of those who know they have much to learn from others."

By this time he was also a part of Disciples-Baptist union talks at the national level, talks that ended unsuccessfully.

Dale Fiers was open to new ideas on how to minister to people. Once, after he heard in a lecture that what alcoholics need first is not condemnation but a drink, he received a phone call from a man who wanted to talk. He met the man, heard his troubles and a plea for money. "How would you like a drink?" Fiers asked him. Stunned, the man responded affirmatively. The Cleveland preacher first got him a drink, then started him on treatment at Alcoholics Anonymous.

In 1947 Fiers was named a trustee of the UCMS, and in 1948 Bethany College awarded him the honorary doctor of divinity degree.

The UCMS elected him chairman of its Board of Managers in 1949. He was remembered by the staff as being able to analyze complex problems quickly.

Fiers took part in the founding of the National Council of Churches in 1950, serving on the council's General Board from that time on. He later headed the nominating committee and program and planning, and was a member of the NCC executive committee.

In 1951 Dale Fiers was called by the United Christian Missionary Society to be its fifth president. He was to serve thirteen years, longer than any other. A second honorary degree, an LL.D., came in 1952, from Texas Christian University. (Culver-Stockton College was to award an L.H.D. in 1957, and Eureka College a D.Lit. in 1973.)

Fiers was chairman of findings for the Committee of 33 that organized the Council of Agencies in 1952, a body aimed at coordinating efforts of the church's many national agencies, and one that laid groundwork for the major Disciples restructure to come sixteen years later. Fiers was chairman of the council in 1956–57.

Feeling the necessity of seeing firsthand the church's far-flung mission effort, Fiers took three months in late 1952 and early 1953 to circle the world, visiting Africa, Europe, the Middle East, India, Thailand, and Japan. This first of several foreign trips deeply impressed him.

He was alternately excited with boyish enthusiasm for the work ("Today was a humdinger!") and depressed by the plight of many of the people ("No wonder Jesus was moved to ministering rather than being ministered unto").

Congolese gave Fiers the name *Bokemyese,* meaning "the one who strengthens the work everywhere." He committed himself early to freeing mission stations to become overseas churches, operated and directed by overseas Christians rather than missionaries and mission boards.

He took a similar position on UCMS work in the United States, favoring unification of work at the state level and the transfer of staff and responsibility to the states, moves that helped develop the present strong regional manifestation of the Christian Church.

In 1953 Fiers wrote a book, *This Is Missions,* based on the diary of his round-the-world trip. In 1960 and 1961 he was to have two others published, on prayer, one a study guide, *Lord, Teach Us To Pray,* the other a lecture series entitled

Prayer and the Great Decisions of Life. In 1966, *The Christian World Mission* identified the changes taking place in overseas missions.

Fiers was asked in 1958 to be chairman of the North American committee of the World Council of Christian Education and Sunday School Association. He later became vice-president of the world body and supported its merger into the World Council of Churches.

The civil rights crisis hit in 1962 and 1963. Fiers led Disciples in organizing a special moral and civil rights committee to raise funds and respond. Later, he was to work hard for the establishment of a major race and poverty program (Reconciliation) in the church, lending his personal prestige by serving as convener of the Reconciliation steering committee. He strongly supported the church's responsibility to speak out on social questions.

In 1962 the Disciples accepted an invitation to be a participant in the Consultation on Church Union, and Dale Fiers became one of the nine permanent Disciples delegates.

As restructure began to develop, Fiers was made administrative secretary of the Commission on Restructure. Then, June 30, 1964, Gaines M. Cook retired and Fiers became executive secretary of the International Convention of Christian Churches, briefly holding three jobs (including UCMS presidency) at once.

A preliminary restructuring step was approved in 1966 at Dallas, establishing a representative assembly in place of a mass convention where everyone who came could vote.

St. Louis was the place and 1967 the year scheduled for the actual vote on restructure. Fiers pushed hard but evidence of unreadiness threatened the vote, and he wisely counseled delay for a year, though eager colleagues groaned.

After the year of continuing explanation, Disciples overwhelmingly voted in Kansas City in 1968 to restructure as a "church" rather than a "convention of churches," with divisions of work as opposed to independent agencies.

Fiers, as convention executive, became the first general minister and president. A year later, in Seattle, he was elected to a full six-year term. He brought unit heads together in a General Cabinet and laid groundwork for the functioning of the new

14

General Assembly, General Board, and Administrative Committee.

Uniquely able to laugh at himself, Fiers has a favorite story that illustrates a communication failure on his part. He arrived late at a convention where he was to speak. It was an occasion when he had to rush in and rush out. The lady registering people in the foyer stopped him to make him a badge. Genuinely feeling sorry for her because it would be more trouble than necessary since his visit was short, he replied: "No, thank you. I don't need one."

But as he rushed by and into the meeting room, he overheard the lady say: "The big stiff. I guess he thinks everybody ought to know him!"

Though he spoke at many regional assemblies, Texas Disciples made an unusual request of him in 1972: that he "be just himself" and not an Indianapolis church executive. He responded by speaking on "Confessions of a Church Bureaucrat," confessing to being a bureaucrat and saying he loved it, because his motivation was love of Lord, church, and mission. Then he played his banjo.

Fiers had brought out the banjo in Indianapolis once at a chapel service in Missions Building and headed a fifteen-minute songfest which he described as doing "my own thing" and which caused a colleague to comment, "Only he could have pulled it off."

A. Dale Fiers has been described by his contemporaries as being always the gentleman, as having first of all—integrity. His every act is couched in concern for others and for "what's right." He has been a steadying influence. His public presence is marked by both poise and humility. (A black Disciple recently told him that she would trade him some of her "soul" for some of his "cool.")

One of Dale Fiers' most remarkable gifts has been his ability to press other people to decisions without hopelessly alienating them. And decisions have been his business for nearly three decades.

Granville T. Walker is senior minister of University Christian Church in Fort Worth, Texas. Since his ministry began there thirty years ago, the membership of the church has increased fivefold.

Dr. Walker was born in Acme, Texas, on October 5, 1908. He holds the B.A., B.D., and honorary D.D. from Texas Christian University, and the B.D. and Ph.D. from Yale University. On graduating from Texas Christian University in 1937, he went to the ministry of the St. Charles Avenue Christian Church in New Orleans. In 1939 he returned to TCU as chairman of the Department of Undergraduate Religion. He became minister of University Christian Church in September, 1943.

In 1958 Dr. Walker served as president of the International Convention of Christian Churches. He then became chairman of the Commission on Brotherhood Restructure (and its Central Committee), which developed the Provisional Design of the Christian Church (Disciples of Christ), under which the church currently operates. Many other church and civic groups have claimed his interest and time through the years.

Dr. Walker is the author of **Preaching in the Thought of Alexander Campbell** and **The Greatest of These,** both published by The Bethany Press.

1

On the Pastoral Ministry

GRANVILLE T. WALKER

IT IS NOT LIKELY that any living Disciple has had a more varied ministry, and more helpful in all its forms, than has A. Dale Fiers. Although some years have passed since he terminated his work in the pastorate for the more comprehensive assignments of brotherhoodwide and ecumenical service, the fact is clear to those of us who know him best that his exciting success as president of the United Christian Missionary Society, as executive secretary of the International Convention of Christian Churches (Disciples of Christ), and subsequently as president and general minister of the Christian Church (Disciples of Christ), were all well grounded in his long service in significant pastorates in Ohio. Indeed, he never ceased to function in the role of pastor and preacher even in the worldwide functions that fell to him, a fact to which I can bear personal testimony, as can scores of other ministers to whom he has ministered. It pleases me greatly to dedicate the following statement to a man who, with all becoming grace and humility, has demonstrated the meaning of the "pastoral ministry" at all its levels.

It is probable that no other centuries-old vocation is undergoing such rapid and unpredictable change as is the pastoral ministry. Books dealing with the changing roles of the ministry come now with regularity from the press. Along with these changes, real and anticipated, and indeed stimulating them, is the conviction on the part of many that the church itself must undergo radical transformation if it is to be relevant to the times in which it now exists. Some of these developments are already occurring on an experimental basis throughout the land, as many young ministers attempt to serve in a pastoral relationship in ways that their forebears would hardly have thought feasible or even desirable a generation ago. Unlike their predecessors of earlier times, young men entering seminary today cannot look forward with solid certainty to what their ministries will be like in a dozen years. "Future shock" is overtaking both the ministry and the church.

Despite these developments, there are certain criteria for the pastoral ministry that currently remain, and undoubtedly will continue to remain, unchanged. For whatever form the church he serves may take, the man called into the ministry of Christ will continue to preoccupy himself with two major functions: (1) knowing, evaluating, and interpreting ideas; and (2) dealing compassionately with people from the standpoint of practical wisdom and Christian concern—both of these from within the context of his own personal faith and commitment to Christ.

The two—ideas and people—are inseparable, even though frequently the pastor finds himself more preoccupied with one than the other, a condition that gives zest and variety to his ministry and saves him from the bane of monotony.

In short, if one has an earnest desire to know all that he can know about the religious faith to which he is committed (and its related disciplines) and which he is to impart and share with his people; if he has a compassion for persons in all their needs and is prepared to make whatever sacrifices are called for in order to meet these needs, he has met the basic conditions of his calling. As John Oman once wrote, the "gifts" (intellectual hunger and curiosity, and compassion) may be the "call" and the call is for the exercise of the gifts.

However measured, personal commitment comes first, for what a man is counts for more in the ministry of Christ than it does in any other calling. A man might be of ever so doubtful character and still be a great teacher of mathematics or science or history. But if he is to impart religious insights and commitment to others, he must *have* and *be* what he proposes to transmit.

What a man is, therefore, is not only first in terms of his qualifications but first as a resource for the pastoral ministry. One's own experience of God, an experience that cannot possibly be mediated through words to another, is the very charter of his ministry. Through some medium—and it may differ from one person to another—the "word of the Lord" must come, saying, "Son of man, stand upon your feet, and I will speak with you." At the very root of all great preaching and all effective pastoral work is a compulsion for the gospel of Christ that has laid strong hands upon the minister's own inner life.

A critic once said of a novelist whose second book was off the press, "He has a style before he has a story!" The business of being a preacher requires first that one have a story, rooted in a compulsion for the gospel that he cannot escape. Style usually comes later. A Hollywood actor once said to a missionary whose sacrificial work on a faraway field had come to his attention, "I wouldn't do what you are doing for a million dollars a year." To which the missionary replied, "Neither would I!"

That is the authentic note of the Christian ministry: We in this ministry are involved in a task for which, as Paul put it, we were "apprehended" by Christ (KJV), which means that he put a hand on our shoulder; he arrested us; we encountered him face to face. And the task is one that money alone could never bribe us into doing. We have this ministry because the love of Christ constrains us. Necessity is laid upon us.

In some such sense one is called to be a minister, but if it is true that the "gifts" constitute the call and the call is for the exercise of the gifts, then others in other lines of work are also "called." Taking a strong view of the doctrine of the priesthood of all believers, Alexander Campbell championed this idea quite urgently one hundred and fifty years ago. Said he in taking to task incompetent and uneducated preachers on the frontier whose sole claim to the ministry was the claim of some mysterious "call":

I am as much called by the Holy Spirit to publish the "Christian Baptist" as any man upon earth is called to preach the gospel. . . . I am led to think from the apostles' doctrine, that the poor widow, or the waiting maid who labors industriously in her station and who obeys Christ, is just as good a servant of God and "minister of Jesus Christ" as ever John Calvin was, or any other preacher or teacher is.

One could hardly get an argument over that proposition nowadays, but it is quite remarkable especially in view of the fact that it was stated so long ago when the Protestant idea of "vocation" as having a religious significance in fields other than the ministry was almost lost sight of. Actually, the Christian world generally has only in recent times come to a fresh emphasis upon the ministry of the laity, that is, to a fuller acceptance of the idea of the priesthood of all believers. What Campbell was saying is the sort of thing that should be said to a young person who wants to serve God but whose talents are in engineering or medicine, business or law. He, too, must be led to see that where his aptitudes and gifts are, he can best serve God. He, too, should be able to say, "Woe is me if I do not."

Those in the pastorate must be sure they can say it. They may hear no mystical voice speaking to them out of the heavens. But they are aware of a divine encounter, of being personally apprehended, as Paul says. They know what Amos meant when he said, "I am a herdsman, and a dresser of sycamore trees, and the LORD *took* me from following the flock, and the LORD said to me, 'Go, prophesy to my people Israel' " (italics added). Such persons have a robust sense of vocation that puts them in the only apostolic succession the Bible knows anything about: "There was a man *sent* from God, whose name was John" (italics added).

The church I serve always has in its membership students preparing for various types of Christian vocations. A few years ago among them was David Luo (pronounced Low), a Chinese refugee who while in school decided to become a missionary to his own people. So he prepared for that, and during the commissioning service in Indianapolis, when the candidates were given the privilege of recounting the reasons why they made their choice (at that time Dale Fiers was president of the United Christian Missionary Society and conducted this service), David Luo simply said: "I always wanted to serve God in one way or another. Then one day I found my name in the Great Commission: 'Go ye therefore into all the world and preach the gospel, and Lo! I am with you always, even unto the end of the world' "—the best of all possible reasons for being in the ministry!

Such a sense of vocation provides the highest motivation for the minister to maintain his own personal moral integrity, apart from which his work both as preacher and as pastor is in vain. What he *is* as a man is more important than anything he does or says in the course of his ministrations. As a preacher he is not an expert in a particular intellectual discipline, transmitting his knowledge to a group of interested listeners, but rather he is a person sharing some of his most intimate and personal experiences with other persons. If he does not know it to begin with, he will ultimately learn that preaching is "not speech about religion, but a religious person speaking."

John Knox, who made that statement, reminds us that although in some religious circles the validity and effectiveness of the sacraments are neither enhanced nor impaired by the moral character of the person officiating, it is not easy to make this point about the preaching. Nor, indeed, about the work of counseling as a pastor. For how effective the minister is depends greatly upon how good and decent he is as a man!

A sense of vocation, issuing in personal moral integrity— this is vital to the pastor in all aspects of his work, whether standing silently and prayerfully with the bereaved, or counseling those in trouble, or proclaiming from the pulpit the gospel of Christ.

Out of his personal commitment, and his knowledge, both intuitive and acquired through the disciplines of study, the pastor deals with ideas.

This means that he must discipline himself in the habits of study, which for some do not come easily but are acquired through laborious effort. To fail to do this is to lack the wisdom to deal adequately and redemptively, whether in preaching or counseling, with the problems of his people.

Preaching provides a prime example. When does one need wisdom more than when he enters the pulpit? Not wisdom without earnest commitment, of course, but wisdom in its most comprehensive sense he needs and needs above all else. For the minister in preaching, as well as in pastoral work, is dealing constantly with ideas. These ideas come not only from his formal academic training and a continuous program of study, but from his constant pastoral ministry to his people, his ability to sense and evaluate their needs, a skill that is stimulated by his compassion and concern for individuals.

Some time ago Sydney J. Harris devoted one of his syndicated columns to a story that had come from London. The George Bernard Shaw memorial committee had disbanded, having despaired of being able to turn Shaw's home into a national shrine for visitors. Instead, the home was to be sold at auction to the highest bidder.

The reason given was that there just simply was not enough public enthusiasm for the project, even though many Britons generally regard Shaw as the foremost English writer of the twentieth century.

Then Harris offered a reason why Shaw was not the sort of writer to inspire a national shrine. Granting Shaw's forthrightness, his often devastating honesty, and that he was highly respected by friend and foe alike, nevertheless, said Harris, "Shaw was rarely able to infuse his writing with the sort of incandescent warmth that makes a reading public feel really close to an author, feel that he is interpreting their own secret thoughts and wishes."

Very few writers can do this, said Harris. Most writers get concerned with "injustice" in general and not with the individual who is the victim of it.

Both the average man and the typical intellectual tend to have faults at the opposite poles of human nature. The average man is warm about individuals but cool toward large ideas. He is stirred by the plight of a Welsh miner trapped in a shaft, but he is relatively indifferent to the abstract injustice in the Welsh mining industry.

Harris went on to say:

The intellectual of Shaw's sort is burning with indignation at the injustice, but relatively unconcerned with the individual miner. . . . Both these views, of course, need to be reconciled. Personal compassion is merely sentimental without general ideas, and general ideas are sterile without a sense of immediate personal involvement. Because Shaw conspicuously snubbed the individual, posterity is beginning to pay him back in kind.[1]

It would be difficult to find a better description of the nemesis of the pastor. Stuck with his books alone, a preacher might find his greatest concern to be with the abstract principles of theology, justice, ethics, morality, world peace, and all the rest. If he becomes heavily involved in social reform (as many a preacher has found himself doing), he can lose sight of the real objective of all social reform: the individual person.

Once Mrs. Humphrey Ward wrote a member of Parliament about a poor family in his district who badly needed help. The

1. Courtesy of Publishers-Hall Syndicate.

member of Parliament had always sponsored social legislation and had put himself on the side of all good issues. Mrs. Ward was astonished, therefore, when he replied: "I am so busy with plans for the race that I have no time for the individual." Mrs. Ward filed the letter with this remark written across it: "Our Divine Lord, when last heard from, had not attained this sublime altitude!"

Indeed, he had not! On the contrary, the common people heard him gladly precisely because he never lost sight of them as separate persons. He looked out upon the multitude and had compassion for them, as sheep without a shepherd.

Jesus' insight is the one most needed by those who would fulfill his commandment, "Feed my sheep!" It is one thing to burn with indignation at injustice in general; it is quite another to be redemptively concerned with the individual victim of it in particular.

No one held these two concerns more nearly in perfect balance than did Jesus. Everything he said is best understood from within the context of his concern for the kingdom of God, that condition of life in which the will of God will be done on earth as it is in heaven, when in all man's dealings with man perfect justice and perfect righteousness will prevail. Jesus prayed, and taught his disciples to pray, for the coming of that situation on earth. But when he told the story of the man beaten and robbed and left to die on the roadside, the whole point of it was the act of individual compassion and concern by the Samaritan, whose devotion to justice issued in a "sense of immediate personal involvement."

The pastor can find no better guide for his own ministry than the ministry of Jesus. His sayings and stories are full of the experiences and concerns of people with whom he was in daily contact.

If one were to examine all that is recorded in the Gospels about Jesus' teachings and ask, "What was the great resource on which Jesus relied?" one would probably conclude that he who spoke as never man spoke did so most often in response to his observation of others' experiences. This is not to omit his own understanding and interpretation of Hebrew religion, his own insights into the character of God and the nature of man, but to say that it all came to focus on his compassion for people and his detailed attention to things that mattered the most to them.

"There was a man who had two sons. . . . " "And he told them many things in parables, saying: 'A sower went out to sow. . . . ' " "If a man has a hundred sheep, and one of them has gone astray, does he not leave the ninety-nine on the hills and go in search of the one that went astray?" "Or what woman, having ten silver coins, if she loses one coin, does not light a lamp and sweep the house and seek diligently until she finds it?" There moves through the Gospels a continuous parade of *people* in varying degrees of need, and of spiritual failure or achievement. And in his utterances Jesus is forever interpreting their "secret thoughts and silent wishes" because of his own "sense of immediate personal involvement."

Here is the important guideline for the pastor—to know his people, their needs, their aspirations, their private inward battles, and to have that knowledge aided and abetted by his knowledge of theology and psychology, of history and ethics, so that both in the privacy of a counseling situation and in his preaching he may deal wisely and compassionately with the needs of his people.

It is this which enriches his preaching more than anything else. Of course, I am not counseling that ministers take the confidences of their pastoral sessions into the pulpit and even so much as allude to them. That would be unforgiveable betrayal. Any listener on Sunday morning who hears his case history laid out even under a fictitious name "to protect the innocent" has a right to question the integrity of the preacher.

On the other hand, no honest pastor can avoid preaching about the areas of human need that are repeatedly brought to his attention through his knowledge of what his people are up against. The need is so pressing that a wise pastor, about once a year, will find it profitable to give a series of sermons dealing with the personal problems that everyone sooner or later faces. The admonition that one great preacher of the past used to invoke upon his congregation is applicable to this area of our preaching ministry: "Be kind to everyone, for everybody you meet is carrying a heavy load." Nobody knows that better than a conscientious pastor.

Year in and year out, the pastor finds that sermons on personal problems are the most heartily received of all the sermons he preaches. The congregation eagerly hangs onto everything he says about happiness, or peace of mind, or anxiety, disappointment, sorrow, fear, and so forth. The great need for dealing with such deeply personal religious problems is underscored by the fact that publishers in the fifties and sixties found a veritable gold mine in so-called religious books in this field, many of which were psychologically and religiously unsound, syrupy, sentimental, escapist. That fact makes it all the more important for the minister to preach about such matters with genuine wisdom and religious insight. For writers in this area, whether what they give out is good or bad, are nevertheless dealing with problems that people are facing. And people are obviously looking for answers. Without too much discrimination, they will take those answers where they find them.

However, the pastor's concern must not confine itself to these personal matters. He must keep himself informed on the great issues that bring about the personal problems of his people. He cannot avoid these issues in good conscience, even though preaching about them may become the most unpopular of his personal involvements in the ministry. Some ministers have found it wise to deal with these problems from the pulpit in the context of other sermons, for people read constantly and are exposed through the media every day to issues of war and peace, poverty, racism, drug abuse, and all the rest, and when they come to church they are not particularly eager to hear a full thirty-minute replay on any of them. In the course of a year's preaching and pastoral work a wise minister can deal repeatedly with all of them and probably with greater effect in the context, say, of the Sermon on the Mount, or the epistles, or the stories to be found in such great abundance in the Old Testament, or indeed the Ten Commandments, the social implications of which are inescapable.

The minister will bear in mind that preaching has two focuses: the Christ of the Gospels who brings personal salvation, and the kingdom of God, which is the embodiment of the gospel of Christ in the social order. These must not be mutually exclusive emphases, producing the pietists on the one hand and the activists on the other, often at odds with each other. Indeed, the major division within Protestantism today is not one that distinguishes the churches by denominations, but one by which Christians put themselves in one or the other of these categories, each thinking of the other as possessed by falsehood and itself as in possession of truth.

Probably on no issue does the pastor's responsibility for evaluating and interpreting ideas, on the one hand, and expressing real concern for the needs of his people, on the other, come to sharper focus, at least currently, than it does on the pietist-activist controversy. His role is not that of taking sides but of helping his people to see that the whole gospel involves both of these approaches to the Christian faith. He is, in short, an agent of reconciliation with his own people—even as he must be such an agent between his people and minority groups —racial, religious, or any other.

Moreover, it is at this point that the relationship between pastoral work and preaching becomes obvious and unmistakable. Preaching at its best is pastoral in nature even when the sermon is dealing primarily with social issues. If we reclaim the oldest figure of speech used to describe the minister's task, namely that of *shepherd,* it is clear that preaching is included in its meaning. The *feeding* of the sheep is an essential duty of the shepherd's calling. Jesus' final word to Peter, the nearest equivalent in the Gospel of John to the Great Commission, was "Feed my sheep."

The nurture of the flock was precisely the task of the shepherd; he was responsible for leading the sheep to those places where green pastures were to be found and water was to be had (meanwhile securing them against thieves and beasts of the fields). Long ago Charles E. Jefferson said: "Sermons rightly understood are forms of food. They are articles of diet. They are meals served by the minister for the maintenance of spiritual life."[2]

The diet obviously must not be confined to milk. It must include, if the people are to be healthy, the meat and bread of serious and vital encounter with the world. The Christian cannot be Christian all by himself. Nor must the minister confine his Christian witness and love merely to other Christians, though John's Gospel seems, at times, to put the emphasis there. To

2. *The Minister as Shepherd* (New York: Thomas Y. Crowell Company, 1912), p. 77.

be sure, he must be honest with the Scriptures and remember that members of the Christian community are commanded to love one another even as Christ has loved us.

The pastor cannot be unmindful in his personal witness and public proclamation of the evils that have been institutionalized in his society and that in some cases bring about, and in others intensify, the problems with which his people and others "not of this fold" are constantly beleaguered. War and peace, poverty and prosperity, race and community all fall within the purview of his responsible concerns. And in the process of "feeding the sheep" he cannot escape dealing, however kindly, with the prejudices that his people nourish and rationalize as good and right. There is often a thin line (continuing the figure of the shepherd) between "protecting" the sheep from the evils of the world about them and "feeding" the sheep on the solid food of Christian commitment and concern so that they are strong enough to withstand and not become a part of those evils, and indeed in order that they may help rid their society of them. It takes courage to fill this role. The shepherd must be willing to give up his life for the sheep. Those who have been ready to do so have made a redeeming impact upon our culture.

One wonders where we would be in the United States today on the problem of race (poorly as we have done) had it not been for pastors willing to take great risks in opposition to those causes which were dehumanizing the people, whether they were of their particular flock or not! Dale Fiers was among those who at a moment of national crisis on racial justice stood courageously with those who dared to protest, and in so doing imparted courage to his fellow ministers throughout the denomination. He was servant to the servants of God, and in this instance, his witness was a witness in act and performance and not exclusively in words, a witness that carries with it a quality of greatness which truly "feeds." It is under such undebatable circumstances that the spoken word comes alive and carries weight.

This recalls the legend of how the doer of a heroic deed was unable to tell his fellow tribesmen for lack of words. Whereupon there arose a man "afflicted with the necessary magic of words," and he told the story in terms so vivid and moving that his words "became alive and walked up and down in the hearts of his hearers!"

You will look in vain for a more accurate description of the work of pastor and preacher than that: a man afflicted with the necessary magic of words, who stands up and tells a story in terms so vivid and moving that his words become alive and walk up and down in the hearts of his hearers.

None is better qualified to tell the story in this manner than the man who has lived it and whose way of communicating it is not in words only but in a life that exemplifies it. It is this which provides the necessary magic of words in the pulpit and the indispensable quality of "personal weight" (as John Oman once called it) of the pastor in dealing with his people one by one. All of us, I would suppose, have heard sermons that violated all the rules of homiletics but which, delivered to a congregation of loyal parishioners who knew their pastor, resulted in changed lives or in a reachievement of emotional stability and a sense of personal worth—not because of the manner in which the sermon was delivered but because the man who said the words had "going for him" the personal weight of his own commitment and understanding.

I love a story told by Joseph Parker of the time when Gilfillan occupied his pulpit in Manchester. "Can I ever forget it?" he asked. "Nothing like it was ever seen under the sun. He took the sermon out of his trouser pocket and laid it in little heaps on the pulpit Bible, and took it up scrap by scrap, and read each scrap at the pulpit lamp as if he were announcing a bazaar or a tea-meeting." So Parker described the process. James Stewart, who recounted the incident, remarked that you could hardly expect any message to survive the handicap of a delivery so execrable. "But listen to the words in which Parker goes on to describe the effect produced: 'First the shock, then the almost-laugh, then the wonder, then the prayer, then the heartfelt thanks. It was very wonderful, and often beautiful exceedingly.' "

As preachers listening to another preacher preach, we too often listen critically, to determine how he does it, what his homiletical paraphernalia and methods are. We are preoccupied with the bucket and the rope and lose sight of the deep spring from which he draws.

That deep spring, more often than not, depends on what the man himself really is, what manner of witness he has borne on those issues most dehumanizing to his and all other people. All of this adds up to "personal weight" which provides the necessary magic of words causing them to come alive and walk up and down in the hearts of his hearers.

This essay began with certain affirmations about the pastor as a man—a man of God who is in God's service because he cannot in good faith give himself to anything else, a man who disciplines himself in study and pours himself out in compassion and whose life gives meaning to his words. The essay ends on the same note, affirming that Dale Fiers has been an inspiring example of these ideals.

David M. Stowe is executive vice-president of the United Church Board for World Ministries, the overseas division of the United Church of Christ.

Born in Council Bluffs, Iowa, in 1919, Dr. Stowe holds the B.A. from the University of California at Los Angeles, the B.D., Th.D., and an honorary degree from Pacific School of Religion, with further graduate study at Yale University.

From 1945 to 1950 he and Mrs. Stowe were missionaries in China under the American Board of Commissioners for Foreign Missions. During the last year he was on the faculty of Yenching University in Peking. Returning to the U.S., he became chaplain and chairman of the Department of Religion at Carleton College.

Dr. Stowe went to the staff of the American Board in Boston in 1956. In 1963 he became head of the foreign missions division of the National Council of Churches, becoming an associate general secretary of the NCC in 1965.

In 1970 he assumed his present position. In this capacity he has had many interdenominational responsibilities through the National Council and World Council of Churches, throughout the world.

Dr. Stowe is the author of **When Faith Meets Faith** and other books and articles.

2

World Responsibilities for American Christians?

DAVID M. STOWE

In 1930 no American Protestant would have questioned the rightness and the necessity of a worldwide effort of Christian witness and service. Even with the collapse of Wilsonian internationalism after World War I, and the sad ending of the Interchurch World Movement of the twenties, the concept of a manifest destiny for the American church, as for the American nation, was still strong.

True, the Great Depression of the 1930s eroded drastically the world outreach of the churches, as missionaries by the thousands were brought home and programs curtailed or closed. But it did not change the assumption that American Christians had a great responsibility for the world; it simply made that assumption less easy to put into practice. When the Second World War was over and the churches were flush with resources again, one of the most dramatic bursts of ecumenical and missionary activity in all Christian history took place in the American churches.

This expression of Christian world responsibility was paralleled by a revived sense of manifest destiny in the whole American nation. Vast schemes of foreign aid and reconstruction, such as the Marshall Plan, and the development of a massive cold war strategy with its implicit image of America as the policeman and teacher of the world, marked the fifties. Then came the New Frontier of the Kennedy era, with its wide-ranging global as well as domestic enterprises in the Peace Corps, the Alliance for Progress, and—the Vietnam War.

Out of that catastrophe there came by 1970 the most radical disillusionment with manifest destiny the American people have ever known. The finest flower of American leadership, brains, and power, bright products of our greatest universities, keen operators of American business, science, and industry, a massive intelligence and planning apparatus, led the nation into such a debacle on a distant shore that the credibility of any American effort to exercise global responsibility was undercut if not destroyed.

Meanwhile there were signs of disintegration in the fabric of American morale and community itself. One missionary in Japan reported that after hearing successive radio reports of the assassinations of John F. Kennedy, Martin Luther King, and Robert F. Kennedy, he could hardly face the Japanese people as an *American* missionary. What possible message or ministry could he have that would not be eviscerated by the failures of the society which he, willy-nilly, represented? Widespread racism, brutal poverty in the midst of plenty, revelations of corruption in public and private life involving the agencies of law enforcement and of justice themselves, epidemic abuse of alcohol and other drugs, and the disintegration of traditional sexual norms were plain for all to see.

By the early 1970s a failure of nerve and an obsessive sense of guilt and inadequacy marked millions of sensitive Americans. Liberal Protestants were among those most strongly affected by this climate of self-distrust. The result was an increasing feeling that America herself might be the neediest mission field and that under such circumstances American Christians had little right, let alone responsibility, to project a ministry to the rest of the world. Statistics of drastic decline in overseas missionaries and budgets document this introversion among the mainline churches.

At the same time the psychology of world responsibility actually increased among fundamentalist and conservative Protestants. In both the secular and religious spheres there seemed to be a self-reinforcing polarization of attitudes. "Fundamentalism" either of the nation or of the church (and often the two coincide) fueled an aggressive sense of American rightness and righteousness which expressed itself in active missions of American culture, power, and religion. Massive bombings over

Hanoi matched massive Bibleings in other regions deemed to be in the grip of the Evil One, who was equally responsible for communism and heathenism.

We shall not examine here whether conservative Protestantism is capable of a critical and self-critical, realistic and contemporary approach to the real issues of Christian world responsibility. There are some hopeful signs that this may indeed be happening, here and there.

Our task here is to deal with the other side of the question, the failure of nerve in so much ecumenical and thoughtful Protestantism.

Perhaps the place to begin is by recognizing a fact. The American thrust across the planet will remain and probably grow through the decades just ahead. At least for our time we shall be inextricably mixed up with the affairs of all the continents and all the seas, simply because we are now the most dynamic and influential society on earth. Even those who cry "Yankee go home" do so with a certain ambivalence because they recognize that the world has a stake in America and America in the world.

No matter what specific political policies an American government may follow, the American thrust into the world will continue. Fundamentalist, conservative evangelical, and sectarian missionaries will go, in increasing numbers, whether ecumenical churches send any or not. American business will continue to be a massive worldwide force. Jean-Jacques Servan-Schreiber, who documented "the American challenge" to Europe's economy in a book with that title, has now decided that American business is about to conquer the Eastern market. An Italian businessman in Russia says that "America comes to Moscow via Italy," as his firm builds American-style supermarkets there using equipment made in Italy under licenses from American concerns. American business investments overseas total nearly $70 billion. The flood of dollars is matched by millions of Americans living, working, and teaching overseas.

In all of this there is a major call to responsible action by American churches. The kind and quality of people who carry this American presence, make its policies, and decide its way of relating to human needs and human potential, will determine the kind and quality of its impact on the world. Many of the American managers, salesmen, and technicians who spearhead and staff the presence of these enterprises are lay people in our churches. Often they are leaders and officers, because they are people of talent and forcefulness. As they weave a net of travel and residence around the planet, they can—if they are properly motivated, oriented, and briefed—do a most constructive job of lay ministry wherever they go.

For that to happen, however, more than good luck is going to be required. The "enabling" of lay persons in world ministries has attracted a fair amount of experimentation since the 1950s. But the going has been difficult. Only the rare churchman seems prepared to see his overseas assignment in terms of Christian responsibility. Yet some encouraging case studies of individual. ministries have been made. The work of one hundred overseas churches with an English language ministry related to the National Council of Churches in the U.S.A., has been substantially upgraded. Many have turned from being chaplaincies to red, white, and blue ghettos to becoming creative centers for equipping Americans to practice a lively personal Christianity east and west of Suez. Many persons are enabled to express their faith through family and personal life-styles, through quiet testimony to colleagues, and through involvement in efforts to make American business, education, and government in host societies a force for social justice and for the self-development of the peoples among whom they live.

North America and Europe are objects as well as subjects of mission: needy receivers as well as givers of a gospel ministry. Few sectors of the world need to hear, obey, and practice the gospel more than the power centers of American life that are noted above—the international corporations, the great multiversities with their overseas academic projects, the State Department and the Pentagon. American leaders who learn something about Christian responsibility in the world while serving overseas and meeting face to face the needs and the potential of other peoples, have a tremendous opportunity to translate those learnings into ministry at their respective home bases.

In this task they can be joined by a multitude of Christians who never physically live overseas: Citizens, for example, who vote not only their conscience but their sanctified intelligence as candidates and parties compete for their support with programs that are either America First or America for the World. Or stockholders who exercise their influence as owners to edge their companies toward enlightened and generous policies in their activities overseas.

In the foregoing the question "World Responsibilities of American Christians?" has been examined not so much in terms of *ought* as in terms of *is*. Given the fact that present American prominence in many spheres of life on this planet is likely to continue for some time, American Christians will either help that action to be humane and moral, to reflect the power of the gospel in some sense, or they will participate, at least by acquiescence, in the opposite. They have no third alternative. For members of our ecumenical churches to cop out, simply to cry havoc at American excesses and failures, to concentrate on domestic priorities and anxieties, will leave the field to fanatics or sectarians in religion, exploiters in economics, imperialists in diplomacy.

Whether we like it or not, the overriding fact about the many branches of the church scattered across the earth is their increasing Americanization. The most revolutionary and renewing event of recent Christian history, the Second Vatican Council of the Roman Catholic Church, illustrates this well. As Catholic scholars have pointed out, what that council did was to endorse doctrines condemned sixty years before by Leo XIII as errors of "Americanism." These included playing down papal infallibility in favor of a more collegial and flexible approach to the teaching function, social activism, enthusiasm for practical and natural virtues in comparison to more specifically "theological" ones, and a predilection for ecumenism.

In many ways these tendencies amount to a distinct "Protestantizing" of Roman Catholicism, a fact noted by many non-Protestants. It is, however, a Protestantizing of a particular kind, not classic Protestantism of the European established churches, not scholastic Lutheranism or Calvinism. Nor is it a Protestantizing reminiscent of that other great sector of Old World Christianity represented by the Anabaptists, Mennonites, or Quakers. This "Americanized" Catholicism is akin rather to an Americanized Protestantism in which the characteristic forms are neither those of the Old World "church" type nor those of the "sect" type, as outlined in the classic analysis of Troeltsch.

"Churchly" Christianity was more or less coterminous with the whole society. It was fully "worldly" in a sociological sense, being linked with the state in mutual service, support, and control, aspiring to a monopoly position in the community, managed by an authoritative hierarchy, and controlled by authoritative dogmas and decrees in parallel and civil authority and civil law.

By contrast, Troeltsch's sect was characteristically "otherworldly" in a sociological sense, entirely separated from the power structures of society, offering an intimate community where pure beliefs and disciplined religious practice could be maintained in relative isolation from the world.

American Christians learned in the New World melting pot to express Christian community in a form quite different from either "church" or "sect," and yet bearing some of the features of each. The American denomination looks something like a sect because it represents voluntary grouping of Christians around particular emphases of practice or doctrine or sociology, in principled separation from state power and patronage. The number and variety of the denominations reinforce this sectarian appearance. Their diversity and pluralism are indeed striking, sometimes all too clearly reflecting narrowed loyalties and vision.

Yet equally clear are certain "churchly" characteristics. American denominations have been at least as much concerned as any Old World church with the general problems and issues of the whole society in which they exist. The sense of being full members of that society rather than marginal sectarians is strong. And in spite of all their variety, the impulse toward many forms of practical unity has been great. One of the most American of all denominations, the Disciples of Christ, arose precisely to try to end denominational divisions by leading a return to the unifying New Testament!

American Christians have generally expressed this impulse toward unity not by striving for a monolithic ecclesiastical organization but by undertaking a wide range of practical activities of cooperation and fellowship. The vast and active network of councils of churches, local, state, and national, is but one example. In undertaking these cooperative activities, American Christians have reflected in religious life a primary characteristic of American experience. Social observers have often noted an enormous reliance upon voluntary associations to get the work of the community accomplished. This habit, no doubt engendered in part by frontier experience, has flowered in the informal ecumenism of American churches.

Christians in communities that are voluntary, plural, free, diverse, cooperative, mutually tolerant and appreciative, democratically governed by their memberships, coveting an active and important role in society at large yet guarding the privacies of free association, providing intensive Christian education to their young in the hope that at the age of decision they will make their own effective decision to continue in the fellowship: this is the characteristic American picture. And this is the characteristic picture of Christianity as it expands everywhere in regions outside Old Christendom. This appears to be due much less to the influence of American missionaries in imposing their own forms on those converted by them than to the congruence of such churchmanship with worldwide social and intellectual currents.

What does this say for the world responsibilities of American Christians? As they have pioneered and lived with these forms of church life, they have amassed a great deal of experience in both their problems and their possibilities. This experience they ought to be sharing with the worldwide community of Christians, warning, encouraging, participating actively in the upbuilding of a planetary Christianity.

We embody and enact our faith in the forms of our community; we also put our faith into words, in order to understand it and to communicate it. Have Americans put their faith into distinctive words, and if so, what relevance have those formulations for our planetary society?

Although academic theology in this country has been almost slavishly imitative of German or British modes, there are in fact some distinctive American ways of theologizing that are highly interesting and possibly important. To set forth the shape of that American theology is one of the more interesting tasks of the 1970s and 1980s. A number of preliminary sketches exist, notably the remarkable statement by Herbert Richardson in his *Toward an American Theology*. Joseph Haroutunian's essay on "Theology and American Experience" is provocative, as is Frederick Sontag's chapter, "Is an American Protestant Theology Possible?"

The most massive example of recent American theologizing is represented by a constellation of process theologians, mostly taking their bearings from Whitehead in his Harvard period, but also rooted in the pragmatists Peirce, James, Dewey, and others. There are varying degrees of linkage between the process thinkers and the earlier native strands of theology, of which Jonathan Edwards is the towering example but in which many theologians, as well as artists like Melville and Hawthorne, share.

What are the salient characteristics of the Christian message as framed in the American way?

The first word is *experience*. American theology has been deeply empirical, not with a narrow reliance on sense experience but with the broadest range of direct human interaction with our environment—natural, social, and even internal. Edwards' preoccupation with "the religious affections" set the style; R. R. Niebuhr's recent exposition of "radial man," man experiencing an intensified total of impacts from his whole universe, suggests the continuity of the theme. Revivalism from the eighteenth to the twentieth centuries, the Holiness and Pentecostal movements (both American in origin), the liberalizing theology associated with Horace Bushnell and the educators who followed him—all of these reinforce the centrality not of dogma, nor tradition, nor theory, but experience.

Pragmatism, that most American of philosophies, focused in the judgment that the meaning of anything is fully contained in the difference it makes in experience. How much that insight drew from American religious thought is not immediately clear, but the connection between pragmatic ways of thinking and American theology and churchmanship is clear and important.

Pragmatism not only reinforced the conviction that experience is central. It focused on a certain kind and way of experiencing—the *active* mode. It asked not simply, What is? but rather, What may be? It not only looked for differences that experience may reveal; it taught Americans to try to make a difference. Like homes on a frontier, values are not so much found as created. Like laws in a wilderness, truths are not just obeyed; they are built. Meanings for life, the perennial theme of all religion, are not only discovered; they are achieved by action. Americans were not content to fathom and adjust to an established order, even on the rare occasions when one existed ready-made. It had no self-evidently sacred status in their eyes. So in theology they did not wait passively to be taught the divine will and way, but rather ventured to help create it. As Haroutunian puts it, "European truth is unveiled as order; American truth is realized as an accomplishment."

All this active experiencing assumed a much wider frame of reference than church and "religion." General experience and action over the whole range of human powers were taken as the primary instruments even for religious understanding.

A Canadian Roman Catholic journal has observed the mood common in the churches of North America that the decisions for or against God, and hence the mystery of faith and salvation, take place above all in the part of life where we spend most of our energies, that is, in our secular existence.

Because the public dimension of experiencing is so important, morals tend to become crucial. One may harbor in private or in conventicles whatever visions one chooses; but to subject them to the tests of common experience and acceptability is to make them very vulnerable to moral judgment (since morality might be roughly defined as the common sense about values which makes life together possible). (Compare the theoretical frame of John Rawls' *A Theory of Justice.*)

If the world and its manifold experiencings is the definitive base for American theology, the primary target is God. American theology has been notoriously theocentric, from the Puritans before Edwards to H. R. Niebuhr and the theologians who prepared the extensive documentation for the Willingen Assembly of the International Missionary Council in 1952. It is, perhaps, a sign of the times that that American formulation of a "Trinitarian" theology of mission, in contrast to the then-prevailing Christo-centrism, anticipated by some fifteen years a major trend in ecumenical theology today. Herbert Richardson has analyzed the meaning of this God-centeredness by pointing out that in the American style of existence a great diversity of experiences, claims, and interests is reconciled in a vast "cybernetic" process of feedbacks and inputs. God is the unifying power of unity in this global and even cosmic process of interactions.

39

At this point two other American characteristics become relevant. One is the insistence upon the right and value of diversity, of plural ways of experiencing God and of perceiving and doing his will. Through many generations Americans have learned an unusual degree of trust in cooperative process as a means to both truth and righteousness. John Robinson, pastor of the Pilgrims, told his embarking flock that doubtless "God hath yet more truth and light to break forth from his Holy Word"—a word always opened and studied in the common life and inquiry of the community. This is an experimental, a dialogical, style of being theological. And dialogue, in the early 1970s, is also one of the new watchwords of ecumenical theology.

If God is Lord of the cosmos-wide process of enacting and finding truth and value, then God is something other than the isolated and static Pure Being or Divine Autocrat of Old World theologies. He is one who is chief in "the Democracy of God," as Walter Rauschenbusch dared to put it. His actions are interactions and transactions with his creatures. His life is sensitive, growing, and even vulnerable. At the same time he is free because he can maneuver within the shifting and growing possibilities of the world process, and not simply enact the necessities of an eternally preordained order. His power is the power of beauty, perfection, immensity, to persuade his creatures to join his stream of purpose; his suffering is exemplified on the crosses where those in whom his dearest purpose finds purest expression are murdered.

But beyond the cross comes resurrection; and in the American experience of faith, hope is vivid. This has been a land of opportunity. American churches have been remarkably "successful" in many ways. It has been natural to accentuate in American theology the fact that Christianity is Good News. The tragic vision has not been lacking, as Edwards, Hawthorne, Melville, and Rauschenbusch all suggest. But faith has characteristically been concentrated on the substance of things *hoped* for. American theology has been the original "theology of hope."

Such is one possible sketch of that theology which American Christians may bring to the world task of the church. Its relevance to major themes in current ecumenical mission and theology has been suggested in each paragraph. American Christianity is already making a major contribution to that world

Christianity which is emerging as the "great new fact of our time." It behooves American Christians to make that contribution actively, critically, thoughtfully, and candidly, sharing the agonies as well as the satisfactions of their own theological pilgrimage.

Yet it may seem ironic to many, and to some perhaps even obscene, that we talk in this way about American participation in the world's life. This is a time when many, both in this country and abroad, identify "American" most immediately with the arrogant horrors of the Vietnam War and the nasty brutalities of racism. Americans' impact on the world has often been destructive, even despicable.

Marine General Smedly Butler told it like it was:

I helped make Honduras right for American fruit companies in 1903. I helped make Mexico and especially Tampico safe for American oil interests in 1914. I helped make Haiti and Cuba a decent place for the National City Bank boys to collect revenues in. I brought life to the Dominican Republic for American sugar in 1916. In China, 1927, I helped see to it that Standard Oil went its way unmolested.

Looking back on it, I feel I might have given Al Capone a few hints. The best he could do was operate his racket in three city districts. We Marines operated on three continents.

The revolutionary logic of American experience, American philosophy, and American religion can easily be frozen into the Neanderthal conservatism of a General Westmoreland telling the Daughters of the American Revolution, "Our own revolution ended the need for revolution forever." Many Americans have an ominous foreboding that Charles Dickens was right when he wrote 130 years ago after his tour of this country, "I believe the heaviest blow ever dealt at Liberty's head, will be dealt by this nation in its ultimate failure of its example to the Earth."

"Example to the Earth"—this is the awful fact against which the question of American responsibility in the world has to be assessed. The power, the influence, the preview of the future that America represents cannot be wished away. The question is whether American Christians can summon the humility, the grace, the energy, and the generosity to play their part responsibly in building toward a twenty-first century which is even now being shaped under the shadow of their great and agonized Republic.

Before his retirement in 1972, **Eugene Carson Blake** was general secretary of the World Council of Churches.

He was born on November 7, 1906, in St. Louis, Missouri. In 1928 he earned the A.B. degree from Princeton University and in 1932 the Th.B. from Princeton Theological Seminary. He has received nineteen honorary degrees, including the D.D. from his alma mater.

From 1932 to 1951, Dr. Blake served congregations in New York City, Albany, and Pasadena.

During the years 1951–66, he was stated clerk of the General Assembly of The Presbyterian Church in the U.S.A., which became, after a merger in 1958, the United Presbyterian Church in the U.S.A. He was president of the National Council of the Churches of Christ in the U.S.A. from 1954 to 1957.

Dr. Blake became general secretary of the World Council of Churches in Geneva in 1966. Thus, he served as chief executive officer at the General Assembly of the World Council in Uppsala, Sweden, in 1968.

He is the author of **He Is Lord of All, Challenge to the Church,** and **The Church in the Next Decade.**

3

The Ecumenical Task of a General Secretary of a Church

EUGENE CARSON BLAKE

THIS ESSAY is a reflection on the ecumenical aspects of the task of American church leaders in the light of the writer's six years of activity as general secretary of the World Council of Churches.

There will likely be very little help given here to any presently active American church leader in determining the specific answers to the specific problems of church strategy or tactics that are presently before him. I hope, nevertheless, that some of these reflections on American ecumenism may be useful to the ecumenical orientation of American church leaders, their critics, and their supporters.

I

A general secretary of a church lives constantly in tension between the interests and priorities of ecumenical structures and programs and those of his church or denomination as such.

Let me illustrate this tension with a problem faced with thirty years ago by my own denomination long before I was responsible for any national leadership in the denomination. It is, I believe, a good illustration because even with three decades of experience since, I am not now sure of what we should have done.

The problem had to do with the church school curriculum of the Presbyterian Church in the U.S.A. Here are some of the relevant facts as I remember them. Our Board of Education was publishing two curricula, one the so-called uniform lessons, based upon ecumenically agreed-upon Bible passages, and the other, graded lessons, also based upon ecumenically determined outlines. The problems we faced were many and diverse. The theology underlying the curricula of the religious education experts in the 1930s was very different from the theology taught to most of the pastors. The educational theory upon which the graded lessons were based was that of John Dewey—even more advanced in some respects than that which had been generally accepted by the public schools. The principal issue was whether education should contain any indoctrination.

There was competition between these official curricula of the denomination and some nondenominational materials more or less based upon the same interdenominational agreed-upon passages, but treated in ultraconservative ways. This competition in sales to the Sunday schools was important to the financial welfare of the denomination's Board of Christian Education. The church as a whole was ready for some kind of change.

We were a denomination fully participating in the work of the International Council of Religious Education, which was the ecumenical agency of the denominations. It soon became apparent that the Presbyterians, though influential, could not persuade the ecumenical agency to act as fundamentally as we believed we needed to act to fulfill our denominational responsibility to our own Sunday schools.

The board, being the agency of a confessional church, believed it ought to provide a curriculum that would enable the local churches to teach the faith of the church. There was a sharp polarization between the "Fundamentalists" and the "Modernists" in most of the churches, and the ecumenical agency was unable to choose a clear position. We felt we had to choose. Then as now, the most important issue was how to interpret the Bible. Our biblical scholars, even the conservative ones, had begun to accept the so-called higher criticism, but we were not in a position interdenominationally to decide to teach it. The issue of the higher criticism was when, and by whom, and for what purpose, had the "books" of the Bible been written. A meeting of the Uniform Lessons Committee had agreed to have a quarter of the lessons on the Old Testament prophets.

Almost all the biblical scholars knew that the Book of Isaiah was composed of at least three sources written by different men, at different dates in the life of Israel. But because the members of the constituency didn't know that (how could they when it was too touchy a subject for most of the denominations to handle?), the committee was afraid that Sunday schools would reject a curriculum explicitly teaching that there were at least three Isaiahs in favor of some "fundamentalist" nondenominational curriculum proclaiming that there was only one Isaiah and that teaching otherwise was to attack the authority of the Bible. The interdenominational committee decided to dodge the question by having the outlines based upon the *books* of the prophets and not upon the prophets themselves.

Under the leadership of Paul Calvin Payne, the Presbyterian board decided to "go it alone." So began the development by the Presbyterians of the Faith and Life curriculum, a project that took ten years to launch and required the investment of several million dollars before anyone could know whether it would be a success.

Some of us went along with this anti-ecumenical move because we felt that truth was at stake, and that the board should teach the Bible as the Presbyterian Church had decided it should be taught in the fifteen or twenty years of fundamentalist-modernist dispute just then ending.

The Faith and Life curriculum, as it happened, was a great success both ecclesiastically and financially. Many local churches in other denominations bought it from us after it was published, but it could not be expected that the education boards of those denominations would sit still while the education board of another denomination "stole" their business. So the Episcopalians and the Southern Presbyterians, and the Congregationalists, who were chiefly affected, then developed their own new curricula and the ecumenical cooperation in this field became less and less important as the years went on.

Were we right to take the bit in our teeth and "go it alone"? We thought we were, and most church educators would agree that we had made a breakthrough in Christian education. But this success was at the cost of ecumenical cooperation.

II

A general secretary of a church will likely make better decisions if he and his church consider the ecumenical structures as being an extension of their own structure rather than alien competitive bodies.

Many American church leaders have what I call "pronoun trouble" here. When they think "we," they too often mean their denomination only. They fall into the habit of thinking "they" when they think of the council structures, whether local, national, or world. This psychological thinking pattern is more important than is often thought. I should hasten to say that national church leaders are often on the receiving end of this same negative attitude of mind of their own denominational constituency. One of a national leader's worst problems arises from the tendency of American Christians to think "we" only of the local congregation and to fail to realize that they are a part of a much larger whole.

The solution to this problem is to involve the top leadership of the denominations in ecumenical decision-making so that its thinking "we" can be based upon reality.

Let me illustrate the problem from recent experience in the World Council of Churches. In 1968 there was a General Assembly of the council in Uppsala, Sweden, which was the last occasion when *all* the top American church leaders could participate in official decision-making by the World Council of Churches. (The next assembly is scheduled for 1975.) At that assembly, some of the American church leaders were elected to the Central Committee, but a majority of them were not. Those who were not so elected (because of numbers) are forced to receive World Council decisions secondhand. Under these circumstances, it is easy for them to fall into the "they" psychology, especially when the decisions are both important and controversial.

At present, there are only 126 members of the Central Committee elected from the 250 member churches in 90 nations. Inevitably as membership in the World Council grew, there were fewer American church leaders elected to this high level of ecumenical participation. In addition, the tendency to elect more youth, women, laymen, and pastors of local congregations to the Central Committee means that fewer denominational leaders can be chosen unless the number of members of the committee is greatly increased. This is financially impossible. Furthermore, in order to secure fuller participation of church leaders of Eastern Europe (chiefly Orthodox) and the continents of Africa, Asia, and Latin America, the World Council found it necessary in 1968 to reduce further, both relatively and absolutely, the number of European and American church leaders on the Central Committee.

These hard realities underline the importance of American church leaders, whether directly involved or not, learning to think of the World Council of Churches as "us" rather than talking of "them" over in Geneva.

III

A general secretary of a church must resist the temptation to disassociate himself and his church from the ecumenical structures when those structures are under attack, especially if the negative feelings are shared by a large number of his own denominational constituents.

In some circumstances there is even public pressure to favor one ecumenical structure against another. For example, I remember an important meeting of American church leaders held at Atlantic City in 1953. This meeting was called by the National Council of Churches to prepare for the World Council of Churches General Assembly meeting in this country in Evanston, Illinois, in the summer of 1954. Nationally we were in the Joe McCarthy era. The American church leaders were smart enough to realize that the World Council of Churches would be attacked by right-wing critics if only because of the fact that there would be in the world assembly some representatives of churches from Eastern Europe. These delegates from communist nations were all church leaders, but the public could not know that some of them were really supporters of their communist governments (whether under outside pressure or personal conviction) and others were in fact deeply critical and enemies of totalitarian communism. Some of us who were in a position to make such distinctions could not do it publicly because of the effect on the non-Communists when they returned to their own countries after the assembly.

The question at Atlantic City was whether the newly founded (1950) National Council of Churches could not somehow disassociate itself from the controversial World Council of Churches. Since most of the churches represented at that 1953 meeting were members of both councils, the decision was finally made that we would stand or fall together, that is to say, the denominations and their American-based National Council would actively support the controversial assembly of the World Council of Churches.

In the years since, there have been times when the positions taken by the National Council of Churches were more unpopular in the United States than those of the World Council of Churches. The leadership of the World Council of Churches has consistently refused to take advantage of such situations that could be detrimental to the National Council.

The most common dilemma faced by American church leadership, as I have said under I above, is whether to "go it alone" or to support fully the ecumenical structures and programs even when they are highly controversial. One would think, for example, that it would be obvious, when acting in a worldwide context, whether in missions or peace-making, that the worldwide structures of the World Council of Churches would receive a priority of support. But this has not been generally the case. Many denominations or confessions have given priority of their time and money to themselves. I realize that when I was general secretary of the World Council of Churches, this was clearer to me than when I was earlier an American denominational official. But despite this built-in bias for the World Council's program, I believe my position is both right and practical. Americans, whether churchmen or statesmen, will be more successful internationally if they support world-based programs in which they fully participate than if they give priority to purely American initiatives and programs. The growing interdependence of our planet demands a multilateral approach.

The bigger an American church is, the greater the tendency to "go it alone"; and the stronger the worldwide confessional structures and operation, the more temptation there is for a church to act confessionally rather than ecumenically.

This is the reason that American Protestant, Anglican, and Orthodox church leaders should be very slow indeed to criticize American Roman Catholic leadership. The Roman Catholic Church is the largest Christian church. In almost every nation where there is any Christian community, there is a Roman Catholic presence. In many places, as in the United States, the Roman Catholic Church is the biggest single church. If one accepts my analysis, he should expect that American Roman

Catholic leadership will be slow to commit itself to ecumenical programs and structures.

However, since Vatican Council II, American Roman Catholic leadership (the Bishop's Conference) has become year by year more and more ecumenical. Protestant, Anglican, and Orthodox leaders should restrain their criticisms and not become impatient; much less should they return to the old anti-Catholicism that was endemic among them for 450 years. On the other hand, Roman Catholic leadership must seek ways to stimulate and respond to Protestant ecumenism in order to carry forward the renewal of the whole Christian church envisioned by Pope John XXIII and the Second Vatican Council.

The church leader who stands firm under criticism of ecumenical structures is a church leader. If he becomes self-protective when the going is rough, he fails in his ecumenical leadership.

IV

A general secretary of a church is tested most crucially when he must make financial decisions and personal commitments of his own time and effort in behalf of ecumenical programs and agencies when the denominational money and his time are both needed by the denomination's own structure.

This testing has been severe in the last five or six years in a way in which it was not in the fifties and early sixties. Although American Christians are giving more money to their churches each year, the increase does not keep pace with inflation. Furthermore, there has been an increasing tendency of all United States churches to spend their money in the local area as against the district, in the district as against the region, in the region as against the nation, and in the nation as against the world. In the face of this factual situation, it is not surprising that national church leadership has tended in these last years of financial stringency to cut back world commitments by at least as much in percentage as they have had to cut their own national denominational programs. This is fully understandable. Viewed from the denominational perspective alone, almost all the American member churches of the World Council have done well. The American church leadership has proved itself again and again to be ecumenical.

But something else must be noted. The whole cost of the ecumenical structure of the World Council of Churches, to be specific, is so small even in comparison to the national expenditures of most of its member denominations that one could argue, as I have for many years, that to reduce ecumenical appropriations by the same percentage as national denominational expenditures does not make sense, especially in light of the expectations that American churches have of the World Council of Churches.

Let me use as an illustration my own church in the late fifties and early sixties. At that time, when the increase of giving had already begun to flatten out after the general postwar rise of the early fifties, the United Presbyterian Church's national benevolence or general mission budget was in the neighborhood of thirty million dollars a year. (It is a much more complicated financial picture than I can here describe and my figures are accurate only for the purpose of general comparison.) Out of the thirty million dollars, the United Presbyterian Church was being asked for a general contribution to support the structure of the World Council of Churches of something under $200,000 per year. I used to argue—then successfully—that it was nonsense to treat that new and creative ecumenical expenditure percentage-wise, either up or down, in relationship to the thirty million dollars. And I still argue in the much worse denominational financial picture of 1973 that such a way of budget-making is still nonsense.

However, it is much harder today to persuade budget committees to act in favor of ecumenical worldwide commitments, not simply because of real financial stringency but also because the whole American culture tends in the seventies to withdraw into itself. We are saying, if I hear aright: "Since the rest of the world is so critical of us Americans, let them try to go it alone without us." Such an attitude affects not only the grass roots but also the denominational leaders themselves.

Equally important as the financial pressure upon the church leaders is the pressure of time. I have attended so many ecumenical committee meetings in the past twenty years that were entirely frustrating that I cannot be too sharply critical of general secretaries (or bishops or archbishops or general ministers) who have decided that they do not have either the time or the energy to go to them. Twenty years ago the ecumenical structures were new and exciting. In the early fifties there was hardly an important ecumenical meeting at the national or world level at which you did not see Bromley Oxnam of the Methodist Church, President Franklyn Clark Fry of the Lutheran Church in America, Henry Knox Sherrill, presiding bishop of the Episcopal Church, and their colleagues present and working hard for the ecumenical cause. I do not criticize their successors. Some of them are equally active and hardworking today. But the ecumenical structures have also grown (as they should in their first quarter century). And even with jet travel, no one can be in two places at once.

Some denominational leaders have solved part of the problem by having ecumenical assistants represent them. But, however able he may be, an assistant cannot make up for the absence of the "head" of the denomination. It used to be said of one denominational leader that he had an uncanny ability to be present at the wrong meeting. That was unfair, as is a great deal of the popular criticism of denominational leaders, most of whom live under a schedule of pressures quite unimaginable to those who have not lived under them. The worst of it is that too many meetings tend to take away time for them either to think or to pray—with disastrous results.

Conclusion

Generally speaking, it is quicker and easier to create denominational structures and to initiate denominational programs than ecumenical. A general secretary is employed by the denomination and therefore has a primary responsibility to the body that employs him. But if he exercises his church leadership only in the light of that responsibility, he is not an adequate leader even of his denomination since, theologically and pragmatically, the ecumenical direction is clearly the fruitful way for all churches to follow. At any particular moment, a general secretary has many a close decision to make between the particular interests of his denomination and the more general interests of the whole church. It is my judgment that, in the long run, a general secretary should make those decisions upon theological and biblical grounds, which are clearly more ecumenical than sectarian.

Ben M. Herbster was the first president of the United Church of Christ, being elected by the General Synod at the very session when the constitution was adopted. He served in this office, which the constitution defines as the minister of the United Church of Christ and the chief executive of the General Synod, from 1961 until his retirement on September 30, 1969.

Born in Prospect, Ohio, on August 26, 1904, Dr. Herbster was graduated from Heidelberg College, Tiffin, Ohio, in 1926 and from Central (now Eden) Theological Seminary in 1929. He served the Corinth Boulevard Reformed Church in Dayton (which he helped organize) from 1929 to 1931. Then followed a thirty-year pastorate in Norwood, Ohio, and from this pastorate he went to the presidency of the United Church of Christ.

Dr. Herbster was an accredited visitor to the First Assembly of the World Council of Churches in Amsterdam in 1948 and a delegate to the Second Assembly in Evanston, Illinois, in 1954; the Third Assembly in New Delhi, India, in 1961; and the Fourth Assembly in 1968 in Uppsala, Sweden.

He holds five honorary degrees (Heidelberg College, Talladega College, Elmhurst College, Franklin and Marshall College, and Lakeland College). He is the author of a book published in 1972, **God Still Makes Sense.** The Herbsters now make their home in Dayton, Ohio.

4

National Church Administration

BEN M. HERBSTER

A MAN who sets out to buy lighting fixtures for his mercantile business follows what at first thought seems to be a very queer practice. He turns his back upon the fixtures and looks rather at the goods that he desires to display. That is the test. Not how the fixtures look, but rather how the merchandise is illumined.

In a sense that is also the test of a good church administrator. He himself is not important, nor how he may seem to the members of his organization. The test is whether the organization continues to undertake, and to perform effectively, the mission to which it is dedicated. Perhaps it is not too far afield to say that a good administrator becomes more and more inconspicuous (though there could be argument about this) the longer he works. The argument would arise because a man who has responsibility in the church for administration has also the added responsibility to give leadership, or direction, to the church for which he is the chief administrator. And really, no matter how much he may try, it is hard for a leader to be self-effacing.

Leadership in Missions

This brings me to the very first point. No chief administrator dares to become so enmeshed in the affairs of administration that he fails to give leadership in the task to which the church is dedicated. I had this brought home to me with gnawing insistence by my best friend immediately after I returned from the General Synod that laid upon me the responsibility which I was to carry for the next eight years. We had been roommates in seminary and had been the closest of friends all through the years. So I knew the affection that was back of the words he spoke. He said, after telling me how glad he was that I was to have this opportunity, "The thing I am concerned about is that you do not get so bogged down in the minutiae of administration that you have no time left to give direction to the way the church should go." I am sure he had me pegged rightly, and I tried never to forget his counsel.

As in the pastorate, there is never time to do everything. It is a distressing fact that when one finishes at night there is always more left undone than accomplished. Letters roll in by the scores—and if one has made a bad mistake (and who has not?), literally by the hundreds. There are always conferences that must be held and committee meetings that must be attended. But, unless one spends time charting the way in which the church should go and then builds the foundations that are necessary if it is to go that way, answering letters, holding conferences, and attending committee meetings will be of little use.

I hardly need to labor the point that direction, guidance, leadership, and balance are so important in the life of the church. In the final analysis this balance must be brought to the fore by someone who sees the whole church and the whole mission and can help make the choices that are necessary. Sometimes it seems to me that this is the most important aspect of the work. When the mission is carried on by different agencies, as is the case in the church, it stands to reason that the executive of each agency will think the work of his board the most important. If he did not think so, something would be wrong.

But as in all church work—and in our home budgets also—there are never enough resources to do everything at once. The most important must be done first, and some of the other kinds of mission must engage in "holding operations." While such decisions must not be made administratively, it is essential that whatever committee must make the decision has the advice of one who, from his vantage point, is able to see the whole operation.

This same overview is important for the national legislative meeting of a denomination (by whatever name it is called). As an administrator I did not try to unduly influence our General Synod. The Synod was in charge and it was responsible for the decisions; but I believed that the Synod had the right to know how the matter looked to me, from the seat where, by its vote, it had placed me. The administrator must be a leader.

Delegating Authority

Another "must" in this business of administration is the willingness and readiness of the administrator to delegate authority to his staff. By himself, he can never complete all that needs to be done. The only hope is that he can gather around himself a staff that will be able to carry out the policies that have been made. The delegation of authority is very important. It means that the administrator not only assigns tasks to other people but then trusts those other people to carry the tasks to completion.

To put it bluntly, after the assignment, a good administrator keeps his hands off the administration of that particular task which has been delegated to another. If the administrator is not going to do that, then he might as well not have a staff. No man wants to be on a team where all the decisions are made for him by some other person. If the job is man-sized, and if the staff person is mature (and this has nothing to do with age), then he wants to have something to say about how he will do the job.

Delegating authority also means that when the staff person has chosen how he will carry out the task, the chief administrator is under obligation to support that person all the way. If he cannot do this, then there ought to be a change in staff. If the staff person, in following the way he believes best, makes a mistake, the administrator still has the obligation to support him. One never tries to get out of the responsibility which belongs to the chief administrator by blaming the consequences upon a subordinate. This does not mean that the staff person cannot be told privately that he made a mistake, and that it is hoped he will do it differently under like circumstances in the future. But as far as the public is concerned, that man is acting for the chief, and, therefore, the success or failure belongs to the chief. I am sure that this is one of the places where mistakes often have been made. It is so easy to try to get out from under criticism when something has gone wrong by saying that John did it, or Jane did it, instead of realizing and admitting that John or Jane was acting under authority and, therefore, the responsibility belongs to the chief.

Discovering and Developing Leadership

This matter of the relationship between the administrator and his staff leads directly to the task of enlisting and developing leadership. Every place the administrator goes, every meeting that he attends, and every consultation in which he engages give him an opportunity to discover people whom he might be able to use in the organization that he administers. This is equally true for all decision-making bodies of the church. The church, like every other organization, has great potential within its ranks; but it tends to rely upon the same group year after year, without enlarging the circle of those whom it enlists and develops. In short, the church needs to involve more persons in the mission, and to this end it ought to discover a great reservoir of persons, talents, and experiences from which it can draw.

Personally, I found this one of the most rewarding of the tasks to which I set myself, but one of the most difficult. I constantly carried a little book around with me in which I would make notations of persons I met who would be likely candidates for responsibility.

There are also other sources for names of those who ought to be drawn into the operation of the church: the regional or state conferences, the associations, and even the congregations. (I must say that sometimes there is a reluctance on the part of the administrators of these regional bodies and congregations to "let go" of their leaders.) I am sure that the church too often has failed to enlist the best people for the tasks at hand.

It is not only a matter of enlisting people, but also a matter of developing those people after they have been enlisted. We learned in the United Church of Christ that the people drawn into organizational work were very much lost in their first year of service. This was true until we began a process of developing the leaders we had enlisted. People do not come full blown either from the "brow of Minerva" or from congregational or conference work. People must learn the outlines of what the church is trying to do, the principles upon which it operates, the mechanics by which this operation is carried to fruition. That

56

takes time, and effort, the kind of effort that must be delegated to one person on a staff in order that he may compile the necessary materials that are to give counsel and check on how effective all these instruments have been. Developing leadership is an important part of the operation of any staff.

These latter years, through the National Council of Churches, it has been possible to enroll staff in leadership development schools, and this has been all to the good. However, nothing like that is available for committee and board members, and so the denomination ought to provide such a service. This is so important that the measure of a church's leadership will depend on it.

The Need to Develop a Team of Counselors

No one man can know everything or see the implications of every decision that he must make. This calls for an administrator to provide himself with counselors. It is a fact that often, just because of the position which the chief administrator holds, information and views available to everyone else are hidden from him. When one sits in the "top seat," people are a bit more reticent than otherwise to tell him exactly what they think. (However, this is not true about the letters that they write. I believe that people will write in poison-pen letters that which they never would have the nerve to speak out face to face.)

All of this underscores the fact that the administrator must seek out a few people upon whom he can rely for the truth about any particular situation he faces. This group must first of all include his assistants and associates on the staff. They have a right to be heard. If they are to be entrusted with the job of carrying out any particular policy, they will be able to do it with better grace and more efficiency if they have been heard and the policy has been discussed with them. Besides, they will have a point of view that needs to be heard. These associates need to be made aware of the fact that the administrator values their counsel and that even if he does not finally decide in accord with their advice, it is appreciated and there will be no lessening of his regard for them if he must decide differently.

The administrator will also need two or three people who have no official connection with his office, whose jobs are not dependent upon his favor, who will have the courage to tell it like it is. It would be good if one of these was a person who does not generally hold the same point of view as his. He needs to be made aware of the rationale of opposite points of view.

The best illustration that I know concerning the need for this small group of people who will say what they think is provided by looking at our country during periods when, because of the popularity of a president or the unpopularity of his opponent, the elections resulted in an almost total lack of opposition. I think the last time this happened was in the second administration of Franklin D. Roosevelt. The number of Republicans in the government was almost nil. I always thought that Roosevelt would not have made as many mistakes as he did in his second administration if, after the British system, there had been "His Majesty's Loyal Opposition."

Be that as it may, an administrator needs to know how the situation looks to other people. And this will not likely happen if he is insulated from the world by his staff, with a prerequisite for membership on the staff being loyalty to the chief.

Personally, I can think of many times when I was kept from making a very serious mistake because I had a couple of people, beyond my staff, to whom I could turn and from whom I could expect to hear the truth, whether it was what I wanted to hear or not.

Now having heard the advice and counsel of others, the administrator will have to decide. The policy cannot be decided by popular vote. He is sitting in the hot seat, "where the buck stops," and he will have to decide. But he must not decide solely upon the advice of the larger or smaller group of "yes" men who inevitably will gather around him. If he does, he will be more vulnerable than he will know.

The Letters He Receives

Every administrator receives a lot of mail telling him what ought to be done and how. By and large, few people write to tell him that what he is doing is good. Usually the only people who write are those who dislike the course of action that he is following. This means that unless he does a little bit of compensating when he interprets his mail, he will likely be led into believing that everyone in the constituency is unhappy with his actions and disagrees with his decisions. This is probably not the truth. The administrator will never be able to be sure of the greater number of people who agree until he has been led, because of the letters, to reverse his field and take the opposite course. Then the people who agreed with his first course will write and accuse him of playing fast and loose with the course that he was following in the first place.

In short, the administrator must always interpret his mail in light of the fact that it is usually the people who oppose the action who write. Those who are for the action seldom, if ever, write. This was borne out in my own experience again and again.

Keeping the Lines of Communication Open

This has a two-part thrust: Keeping the lines of communication open to the staff and keeping the lines of communication open to the people—the members of the church.

First, the men who have responsibility to the administrator have a right of access to him, in order that they may check their own judgment against his; report the progress that they are making in solving the particular problems referred to them; consult with him about the next steps; and receive a little encouragement in days when the going is rough. I say frankly that if I were working on a staff and the chief of that staff were ordinarily and habitually too busy to see me, I would begin to look elsewhere for a job. Generally speaking, the staff knows that the chief is busy, and when members think it is important enough to break into that "busyness," then the chief needs to have time for them.

Second, during these times all members of the establishment are under suspicion. This means that an administrator must be all the more eager to keep open the lines of communication to the membership. How will he be able to serve the people unless he knows their needs, and how can he know those needs unless they feel free to write to him, to speak with him, about what they think ought to be done? No one man or staff has all the answers. This means that the administrator must be available at all times for consultations, conversations, criticisms, discussions.

Whether that consultation is of worth or not will depend upon whether the people believe the administrator is approachable and warmhearted. It is easy for the chief to become so concerned about the minutiae of administration that he shunts away those from whom he could learn the most. An administrator is also in danger of not listening when he is being spoken to but rather thinking ahead to the problems that next need to be tackled. It is as true of an administrator as it is of a pastor that if he is invisible through the week he will be incomprehensible on Sunday. This means that the administrator must be around and about the whole church, large congregations and small ones, so that the people will know that he is concerned about them, and that he will consider what they think needs to be done.

Probably the years in which I was chief administrator of the United Church of Christ were unusual years because the denomination was just getting started, but I received more thanks for my availability to the churches when the churches had need than for anything else. Likely it is not as important now as it was then, but then it was most important. In a sense it will always be important.

The Ability to Say No

Anyone can be popular if he gives to all comers what they want. The mark of greatness is to be able to say no to the unreasonable and unjust demands of people and to make that no stick, and in the end to have as little divisiveness as possible result from these disappointed petitioners. I put no little emphasis here on the ability to say no and to make it stick. It would be sheer agony, to say nothing of frustration, to work for or with one who was always changing his decision once it had been made.

Now, of course, this does not mean that decisions should never be changed. That would be stupidity compounded. But a chief administrator does have responsibility to his staff to continue a decision once it has been arrived at, no matter how much pressure is brought to bear by those who are in disagreement with the decision. If the staff has reason to believe that, without regard to the morality of the situation, the policy will be scrapped if enough negative opinions are offered, then the morale of that staff will be constantly in jeopardy. So the administrator must firmly, but kindly, follow a course to the conclusion once it has been set.

When Will the Chief Speak for the Church?

This is without a doubt one of the most delicate questions that will have to be faced. On this issue the chief administrator cannot help being aware that there are two schools of thought and it is impossible to please both of them. One school says that an administrator dare never speak out unless he has the majority (usually the overwhelming majority) of the church behind him. This really means that he will never speak out, for in free churches it is very difficult, if not impossible, to ascertain what the majority stands for. A plebiscite seems very impractical.

The other school of thought maintains that as a leader he is responsible for giving leadership and this includes speaking out concerning what is right and wrong, as life looks to him. I wish it were possible to suggest ways in which these two points of view, each held by sincere people, could be reconciled.

There is yet a third aspect of this issue, which is responsible for no little confusion. The press is always looking for a story; and when it finds one in which an administrator makes a statement as an individual, the press is not always careful to make it plain that he was speaking as an individual, not as an administrator. He may make a statement a page long, which he begins and ends with a caveat that he speaks not for his organization but as a private citizen, or as an individual Christian. However, when that statement greets the light of day in tomorrow's paper, it may be two sentences long (and the most controversial sentences at that), without any implication that he was not speaking as chief administrator of such and such church. I am not criticizing the press. The job of the press is to get a story that will attract attention. I am only telling it as it is.

There are people who believe that it is impossible for a man to separate himself from his job, and that, therefore, the administrator must always seal his lips unless he has a clear mandate from the great majority of the people. Even a vote of the General Synod or the General Council seldom (or never) does that. In short, under this idea, an administrator dare never speak out.

I once received a letter from one of my friends, a copy of which he sent to the *United Church Herald* for its column, in which he criticized me for a position I had taken, when the press had actually made it clear that I was not speaking for the church. I wrote him in what I hoped was as friendly a tone as he had written me. I said that I had paid too high a price for the office of president of the United Church of Christ if, by my election, I had forfeited the right to speak out frankly and honestly, of course always making certain that I stated clearly when it was my own opinion and not that of the church.

As to how this course that is filled with so many pitfalls can be charted, I have no advice except to say that words will have more weight if one does not speak out too often, but only when he feels he cannot in good conscience keep quiet.

Strengthening Personal Resources

An administrator must never get so busy doing what must be done that there is no time left for anything else. No one expects an administrator to work twenty-four hours a day or seven days a week or three hundred sixty-five days a year. If he tries it he will, in the end, be of little worth. He should get away from his job on a regular basis so that he will have time to do some things that are even more important. Unless he does, the rest of his work will not matter much.

There are three applications of this, and I give them in ascending importance. First, an administrator needs to get away so that there is time for some diversion, recreation, and rest. "All work and no play" takes its toll not only in boys but in administrators. I know all about the pressure of the job and how, even if one works all the time, he will not get finished. However, there is nothing that brings a person back to the job with new enthusiasm and zest as a little time off. I also know that unless one plans for those times, he will never find time for them. So he must be as faithful to the days that he marks off on his calendar for recreation and refreshment as he is to the days that he saves for committee meetings and speeches.

The second application has to do with time for thinking, planning, and analyzing. This cannot be done if an administrator concerns himself, all the time, with the thousands of interruptions that necessarily plague his days. He must get away more than occasionally in order to measure what he has done, what he should do, and what are the goals ahead. Too many administrators fail here. They fail because the pressure of answering the phone and replying to correspondence is great, but no one presses them to do any evaluating or planning. The daily tasks have to be done—but not at the expense of long-range planning and thinking. The chief administrator owes it to the church that has committed to him the task of administration to come back to the work with a new determination of what is priority number one for him and for his staff—in fact for the whole church. And to make these decisions he must have time. Just as the administrator has to determine what ought to be the priorities for the church, so he must also decide what are his own priorities. One cannot fight on all fronts at the same time. One cannot spread himself too thin and continue to make any impact at all upon the church. He must decide to what he is going to devote himself today and tomorrow. This is a continuing decision. But there is little that is more important.

The third application of this has to do with his own spiritual life. The fact that he is a church administrator is no reason why his devotional life will automatically be at its best. But if he is going to do a job well, his devotional life must be at its best. Christ will be his friend only if he takes time to nurture that friendship. *So he must never be too busy* to worship, meditate, and pray. If he thinks he is, then he is too busy to be an administrator. The job of leading and guiding a church is too important and too difficult to do alone. He must walk with his Lord, and he must follow the disciplines that will allow Christ to walk with him. *These disciplines are so important that one neglects them at his peril.*

A Good Administrator

These are surely not the only prerequisites for an administrator, but they are enough to set our minds at work. Like the editors of this volume, I do not want to make this chapter sentimental. No man alive can fulfill all of what I have written here, to say nothing of doing it perfectly. But Dale Fiers has been and is a good administrator as judged by the qualities I have outlined. His work has been excellent during difficult, very difficult, days. The Christian Church is different because of his administration and it is different in the right direction. All of us have been blessed to know and work with him, and in this simple way we would say "thank you."